Table of Cont...

Tools & Materials

There's more than one way to bring forest animals to life on paper—you can use crayons, markers, colored pencils, or even paints. Just be sure you have plenty of good animal colors—yellows, reds, grays, and browns.

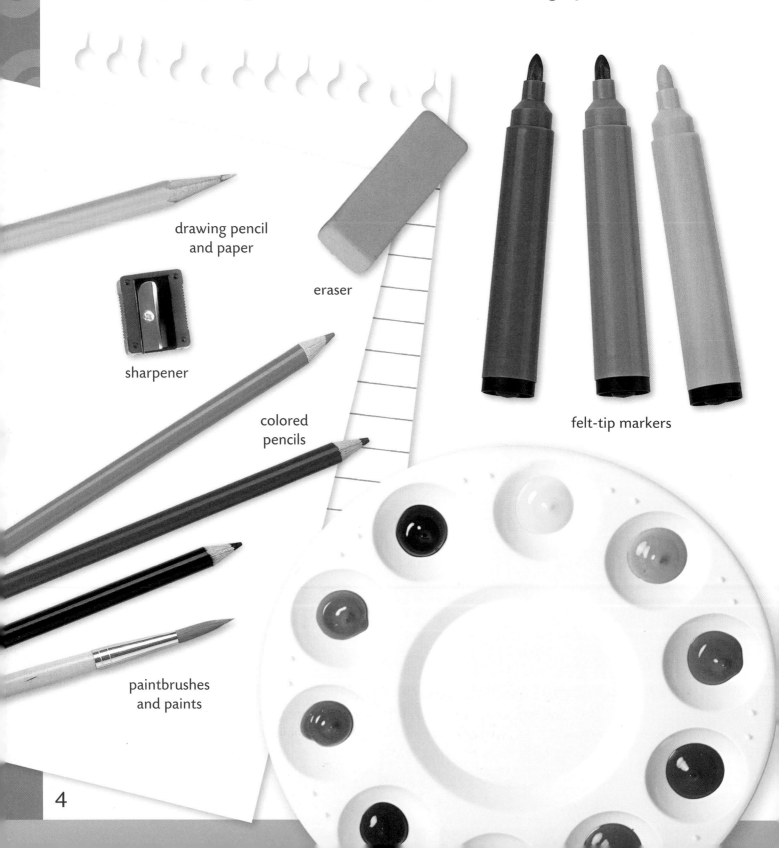

drawing pencil and paper

eraser

sharpener

colored pencils

felt-tip markers

paintbrushes and paints

How to Use This Book

The drawings in this book are made up of basic shapes, such as circles, triangles, and rectangles. Practice drawing the shapes below.

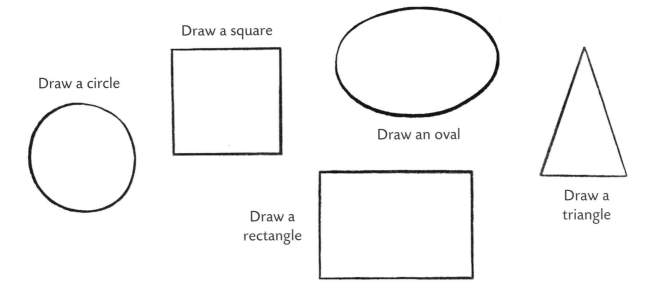

Draw a square

Draw a circle

Draw an oval

Draw a rectangle

Draw a triangle

Notice how these drawings begin with basic shapes.

In this book, you'll learn about the size, weight, location, diet, and appearance of each featured animal of the forest. Look for mini quizzes along the way to learn new and interesting facts!

Look for this symbol, and check your answers on page 64!

Vocabulary

When learning about animals of the forest, you may come across some terms you don't know. Learn the words below so you can better understand the animals as you read this book!

Nocturnal: An animal that is active mainly during the nighttime hours.

Hoofed: An animal with hard, horn-like coverings over the feet. Hooves are made of *keratin*—the same material as our fingernails!

Mammal: A warm-blooded animal with hair or fur that gives birth to live babies rather than eggs.

Antlers: Horn-like bones that protrude and branch from the front of an animal's head. Antlers help animals defend themselves, prove themselves strong, and attract mates. Animals, such as male deer, shed their antlers every year.

Adaptable: An animal that adjusts well to changing conditions or surroundings.

Grizzled fur: A coat of fur that is sprinkled with gray.

Horns: Horns are one-pointed growths of keratin. Animals do not shed their horns; in fact, horns continue to grow throughout an animal's lifetime. Like antlers, horns are used to show dominance and help with self-defense.

Rodent: An order of animals that lack canine teeth but have strong *incisors* (or front teeth). These incisors grow throughout a rodent's entire life!

Venomous: An animal that is capable of harming others with a poisonous substance.

Bald Eagle

Details

Size: 43 inches long
Weight: Up to 14 pounds
Diet: Fish, crabs, snakes, and birds
Location: North American lakes, rivers, and coasts

Did You Know?

The bald eagle is both a scavenger and skilled hunter that uses its powerful talons to pluck fish from the water.

The majestic bald eagle has piercing yellow eyes, a head covered in white feathers, and an impressive wingspan of more than 6 feet.

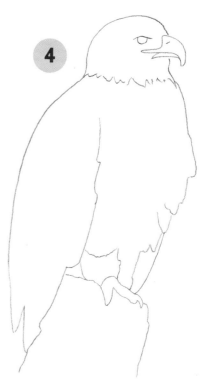

Fun Fact!

The bald eagle is the national bird of the United States of America.

Barn Owl

Size: 16 inches long

Weight: Less than 2 pounds

Location: Every continent except Antarctica

Diet: Rodents

Did You Know?

Barn owls make a range of noises from screeches to hisses, but they do not "hoot" like other owls.

The barn owl has small, dark eyes and a heart-shaped face. These adaptable birds make their homes in buildings and hollow trees.

1

2

3

Mini Quiz

WHich of the following is NOT a barn owl color?

A. Yellow
B. orange
C. Black
D. White

(Answer on page 64)

4

5

6

Bighorn Sheep

Location: Western North America

Size: Up to 42 inches tall at the shoulder

Diet: Grasses, shrubs, and other plants

Weight: 155 to 300 pounds

Did You Know?

A male's horns continue to grow until he is 8 years old. The horns alone can weigh as much as 30 pounds!

12

Bighorn sheep have very large, curling horns and hoofed feet that help them walk on rocky terrain. They also have white patches of fur on their rumps.

Mini Quiz

True or False: Male bighorn sheep (called "rams") have horns, but females (called "ewes") do not.

(Answer on page 64)

Bison

Details

Size: 5 to 6.5 feet tall at the shoulder
Weight: 700 to 2,000 pounds
Diet: Grasses, herbs, and other plant matter
Location: North American plains and European woodlands

Did You Know?

European bison were once extinct in the wild! However, in the second half of the 20th century, zoo bison were reintroduced into nature and currently exist in herds across Eastern Europe.

14

Often called a "buffalo," a bison is a hoofed beast with humped shoulders, a shaggy brown coat, and a mane of hair around its neck and head.

Fun Fact!

Both male and female bison have short horns that curve upward.

Bobcat

Details

Size: Up to 40 inches long
Weight: Up to 30 pounds
Diet: Rabbits, mice, birds, and small game
Location: North America

Did You Know?

The bobcat's fur coat ranges from gray and beige to red-orange and brown.

Bobcats are solitary felines with excellent hunting skills. They have beautiful black-spotted coats, long cheek fur, big paws, and tufted ears.

The bobcat's name comes from its short, stubby tail, which looks cropped or "bobbed."

Fun Fact!

Chipmunk

Details

Size: 8 to 11 inches long (including tail)
Weight: 1 to 5 ounces
Diet: Seeds, berries, grains, nuts, and insects
Location: North America and Siberia

Did You Know?

A chipmunk's cheek pouches expand, allowing it to carry seeds and nuts to its home where it stores food for the winter.

Chipmunks are small squirrels with big eyes, bushy tails, and stripes that run over their faces, backs, and tails. They can be found on forest floors or up in the trees.

Least chipmunks of North America are the smallest in the world. They are about 7 inches long and weigh just an ounce.

Fun Fact!

1

2

3

4

5

6

Coyote

Size: 24 inches at the shoulder

Diet: Fruit, grass, and a wide variety of animals

Location: North and Central America

Weight: up to 50 pounds

Did You Know?

The coyote is mostly nocturnal. If a pack is nearby, you may hear their distinct howls and yelps as they hunt at night.

20

These quick and clever canines have downward-pointing tails and triangular ears. Found in a variety of environments, coyotes are skilled hunters with keen senses.

Mini Quiz

Which of the following is part of a coyote's diet?

A. Deer
B. Insects
C. Frogs
D. Birds
E. All of the above

(Answer on page 64)

21

Cutthroat Trout

Details

Size: 8 to 20 inches long
Weight: 9 pounds
Diet: Insects, worms, small fish, and fish eggs
Location: Western North America

Did You Know?

Although most are found in freshwater, such as rivers and lakes, the cutthroat trout can also travel to and from ocean water.

The cutthroat trout has silvery or golden skin with black spots.
This fish gets its name from the red streaks that run beneath its mouth.

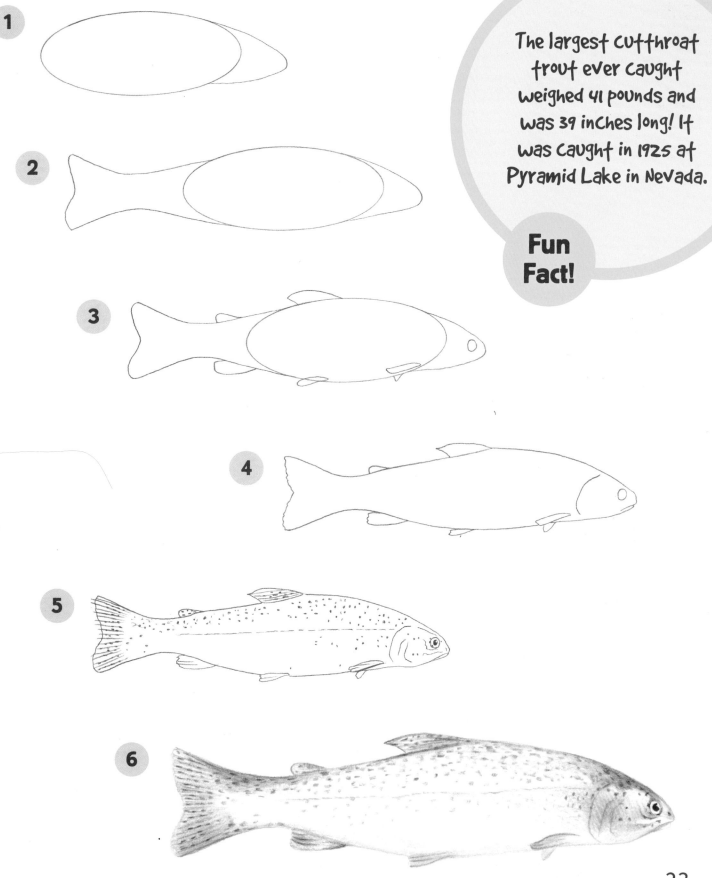

The largest cutthroat trout ever caught weighed 41 pounds and was 39 inches long! It was caught in 1925 at Pyramid Lake in Nevada.

Fun Fact!

Fawn

Did You Know?

Fawns develop very quickly. They don't move around much during their first few days of life, but by one week they can run and by two weeks they can start eating plants!

A fawn is a young deer that is less than one year old.
It has long, gangly legs and white spots on its coat that fade as it matures.

Fun Fact! fawns are born in late spring through early summer so that they have plenty of food available to eat as they grow.

Forest Elephant

Size: 6 to 10 feet tall at the shoulder

Diet: Grasses, leaves, roots, and fruit

Location: African rainforests

Weight: 2,000 to 6,000 pounds

African forest elephants are a different species from the African bush elephants that roam the grasslands. forest elephants are smaller in size and have thinner, straighter tusks.

Did You Know?

With a giant body, brownish-gray skin, thick legs, and a long, powerful trunk, the forest elephant is one of earth's largest land mammals.

Mini Quiz

How many years can a forest elephant live?

A. 10 years
B. 20 years
C. 50 years
D. 70 years

(Answer on page 64)

27

Gray Squirrel

Details

Size: Up to 2 feet long (including tail)
Weight: 1 to 3 pounds
Diet: Nuts, seeds, bark, berries, flowers, and insects
Location: North America

Did You Know?

Gray squirrels don't just live in the forest. These adaptable rodents have adjusted well to humans and can be found in city parks and neighborhoods!

This alert little creature has perky ears, a pointed face, and round eyes. It is known for its gray, white, and tan grizzled coat and long, bushy tail that curls upward.

Fun Fact! The gray squirrel is an arboreal animal, which means that it lives among the trees. They have small but strong, sharp claws that make them quick and agile climbers.

Grizzly Bear

Diet: Berries, roots, bulbs, shoots, fish, rodents, and small hoofed animals

Size: Up to 8 feet long

Location: North America

Weight: Up to 900 pounds

Fun Fact!

The grizzly bear has great hearing and an even more impressive sense of smell. This bear can scent its prey from up to 18 miles away!

The grizzly bear is a large, aggressive brown bear with a shaggy coat and humped shoulders. This feared predator has a powerful jaw and long claws.

1

2

Mini Quiz

True or false:
The grizzly bear is the largest bear on the planet.

(Answer on page 64)

3

4

5

6

31

Hedgehog

Size: Up to 1 foot long

Diet: Insects, worms, reptiles, centipedes, and mice

Location: Europe, Asia, and Africa

Weight: 1.5 to 2 pounds

The hedgehog gets its name from the range of hog-like sniffing sounds it makes while grazing the forest floor in search of food.

Did You Know?

The hedgehog is a small mammal with a coat of sharp spines and a pointed nose. It protects itself from predators by curling up into a ball and raising its spines.

Mini Quiz

True or false: A hedgehog's spines cover its entire body.

(Answer on page 64)

33

Mountain Lion

Size: 6.5 feet long (including tail)
Weight: Up to 130 pounds
Diet: Deer, coyotes, rabbits, bobcats, raccoons, and other small prey
Location: North and South America

Did You Know?

The mountain lion is a stealthy predator that hunts by stalking and surprising its prey. once the lion has made a kill, it often hides the carcass from other animals and feeds on it for a period of several days.

34

Found in a range of habitats, this wildcat is a solitary animal with powerful legs, large paws, rounded ears, and a long, dark-tipped tail.

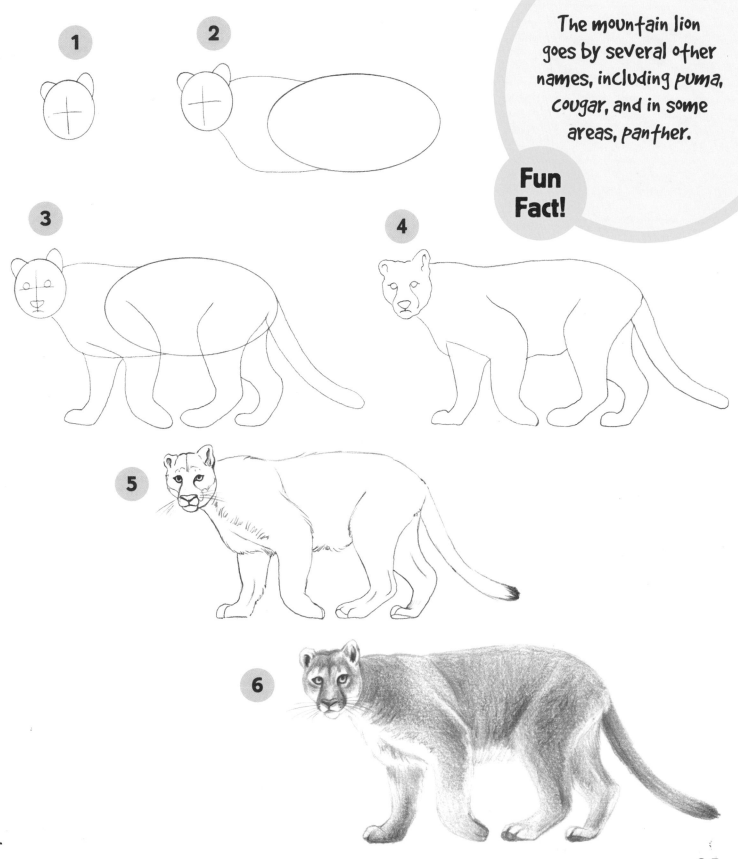

The mountain lion goes by several other names, including *puma, cougar,* and in some areas, *panther.*

Fun Fact!

Mute Swan

Diet: Aquatic vegetation, insects, worms, frogs, and small fish

Size: 50 inches long

Location: Great Britain and Ireland

Weight: 20 to 25 pounds

Fun Fact!

Baby mute swans (called "cygnets") hatch from their eggs wearing a coat of grayish brown feathers. Around one year of age, their coat of feathers will be completely white.

Mute swans are graceful white birds of the British Isles. They have long necks, black facial markings, sharp senses, and great memories.

Mini Quiz

What are the names for male and female mute swans?

A. Cobs and pens
B. Bucks and does
C. Bulls and cows
D. Dames and stags

(Answer on page 64)

Orangutan

Did You Know?

An orangutan's arms are much longer than its legs. In fact, an orangutan's impressive arm span reaches 7 feet across. Their powerful arms help them swing effortlessly among the trees.

38

The orangutan is a large primate with a wide, flat face and a coat of dark orange hair. This tree-dwelling creature is the only great ape that lives in Asia.

Fun Fact!

In the Malaysian language, the word orangutans means "people of the forest." In fact, these intelligent beings are one of the closest relatives of humans and are even known to use tools!

Pileated Woodpecker

Details

Size: Up to 19 inches long
Weight: 10 ounces
Diet: Carpenter ants, beetle larvae, nuts, and fruits
Location: North America

Did You Know?

Woodpeckers have long, strong bills and sticky tongues. These traits help them break through tree bark and pull out ants and larvae. They also quickly tap their bills on wood as a way of claiming territory and calling mates.

The pileated woodpecker is known for the tapping sounds it makes against wood in search of food. It has a black body, white head stripes, and a red crest of feathers.

The pileated woodpecker creates large holes in wood that later serve as nests for other animals such as owls.

Fun Fact!

Stag

Size: Up to 5 feet at the shoulder

Diet: Leaves, shoots, twigs, nuts, flowers, and fruit

Location: North America, South America, Europe, Asia, and Africa

Did You Know?

Every spring, a stag's antlers have a soft, velvet-like covering that nourishes and protects growing antlers. In the fall, stags rub off the velvet, and the antlers stop growing.

Weight: 500 pounds

A stag is a large male deer with an impressive set of antlers. Compared to a female deer, the stag has a sturdier appearance with a thick neck and a mane of hair.

1

2

3

4

5

6

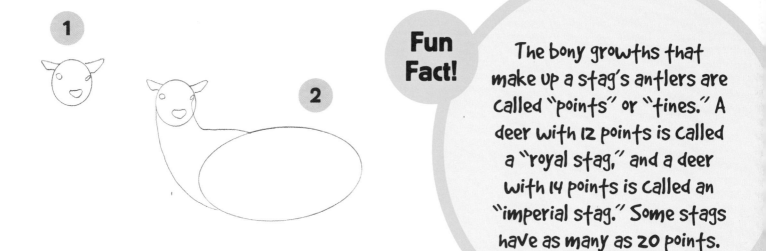

Turkey

Size: 50 inches long
Weight: Up to 20 pounds
Diet: Seeds, insects, snails, frogs, and small reptiles
Location: North America

Did You Know?

The turkey is known for its beautiful plumage, or feathers. Males (called "gobblers") have more extravagant feathers than females (called "hens"). Males also fan their tails and puff up their feathers to appear larger when courting females.

The turkey is a large bird with a red *snood* (flap of skin over the beak) and a red *wattle* (fleshy pouch over the neck). Turkeys fly short distances and sleep in trees.

Fun Fact!

The skin color of a male turkey's head changes depending on its mood. A red head can mean that he wants to fight, whereas a blue head means he's simply excited.

Gray Wolf

Details

Size: 30 inches tall at the shoulder
Weight: 100 pounds
Diet: Hoofed animals, small mammals, birds, reptiles, and fruit
Location: North America, Eurasia, and Africa

Did You Know?

Gray wolf coats range widely in appearance. They can be white, black, gray, tan, reddish-brown, or any combination of these colors. Wolves that live in Arctic regions are usually light in color, which helps them blend in with the snow.

The gray wolf is a cunning canine with triangular ears, a strong jaw, and a bushy, tapering tail. It lives in packs of up to 10 wolves and communicates through howls.

Also called "timber wolves," gray wolves are larger than any other canine on earth. Their bodies can be up to 6.5 feet long.

Fun Fact!

Beaver

Details

Size: Up to 30 inches long (excluding tail)
Weight: Up to 60 pounds
Diet: Inner tree bark, leaves, twigs, and aquatic vegetation
Location: North America, Europe, and Asia

Did You Know?

Beavers are quite the craftsmen! They cut and use wood to build homes (called "lodges") and dams, which pool water to both protect their homes and provide an area for vegetation to grow.

Beavers are large rodents that make their homes along the banks of rivers, ponds, and lakes. They are known for their large, sharp front teeth that cut through wood.

Beavers are adapted to a watery lifestyle. They have webbed back feet, paddle-like tails, and oily, water-repellent coats.

Fun Fact!

Moose

Size: Up to 7 feet tall at the shoulder

Location: North America, Europe, and Asia

Weight: 500 to 1,300 pounds

Diet: Grasses, shrubs, mosses, lichens, pinecones, and aquatic plants

The moose has a flap of skin hanging from its chin and throat called a "bell" or "dewlap." Males have larger bells than females, but still no one is sure of a bell's purpose!

Did You Know?

The moose has very tall legs, humped shoulders, and a downward-sloping nose. Males also have a set of wide, flat antlers.

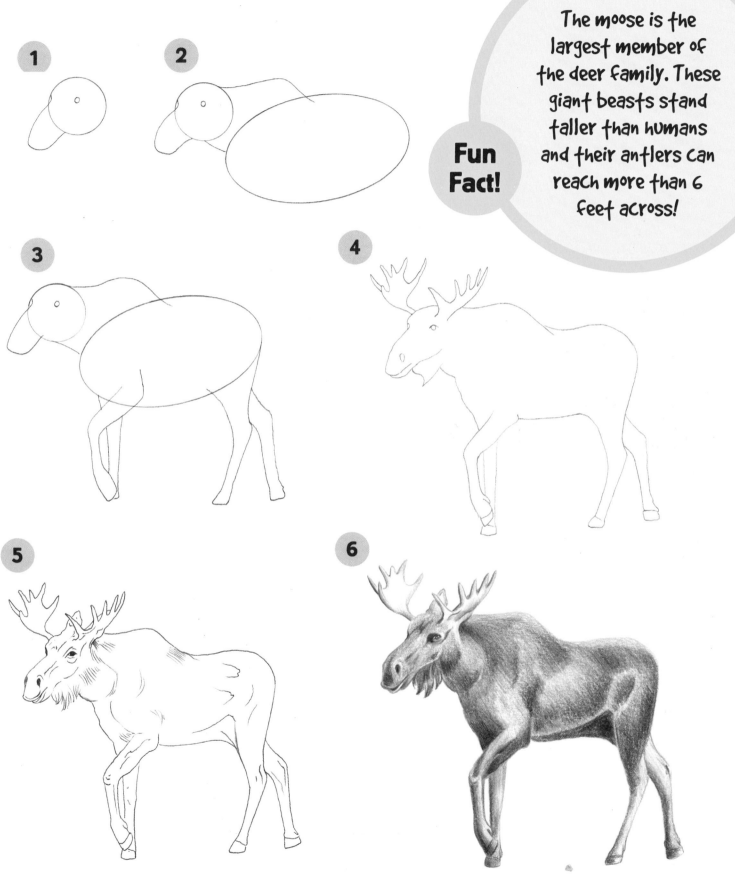

Fun Fact!

The moose is the largest member of the deer family. These giant beasts stand taller than humans and their antlers can reach more than 6 feet across!

Pine Marten

Details

Size: 14 to 20 inches (excluding tail)
Weight: 2 to 4 pounds
Diet: Rodents, insects, birds, fish, reptiles, fruits, berries, and nuts
Location: North America, Europe, and Asia

Did You Know?

Pine martens are members of the weasel family and have coats ranging from gray to yellow to dark brown. They also have light chest and throat markings called "bibs."

These adorable forest dwellers have triangular faces, long necks and bodies, and bushy tails. They have sharp claws designed for quick climbing.

Fun Fact!

In the winter, pine martens have to hunt creatively! These resourceful critters are known for finding prey within tunnels of deep snow.

Prairie Rattlesnake

Size: 3 to 4 feet long

Weight: 1 pound

Location: North and South America

Diet: Rodents, birds, rabbits, and reptiles

Did You Know?

Rattlesnakes are definitely dangerous creatures, but they don't attack unless they've been disturbed or threatened. Despite their venomous bites, the rattlesnake causes fewer deaths per year than bee stings!

Also called the "western rattlesnake," the prairie rattlesnake is a venomous snake with a triangular head, a forked tongue, a brown body, and a rattle at the end of its tail.

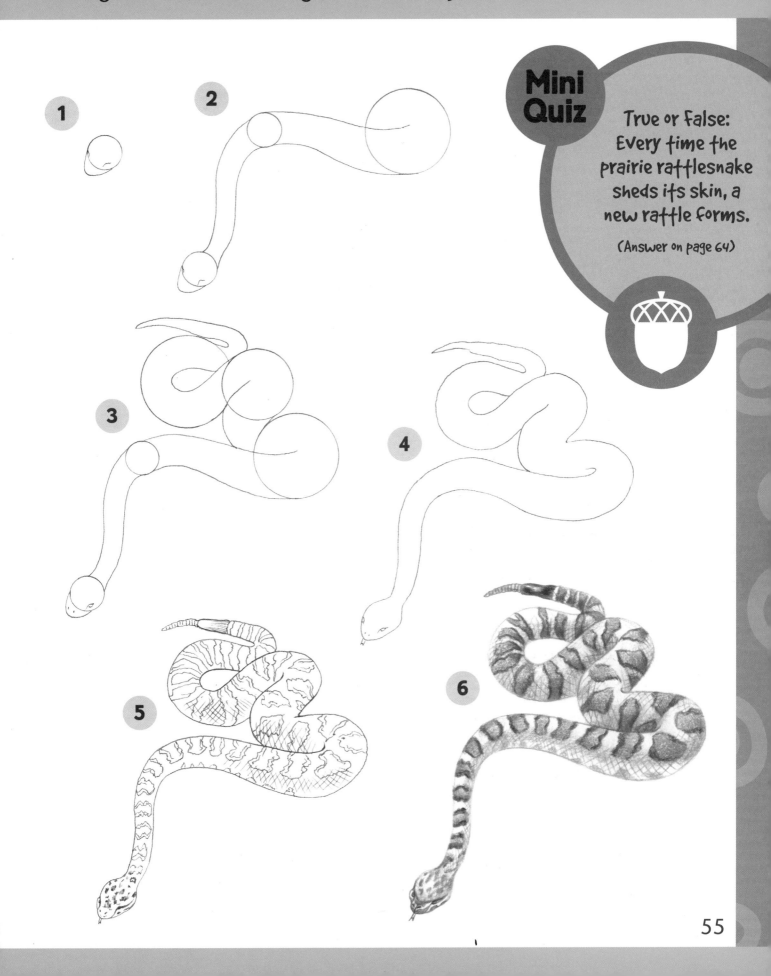

Mini Quiz

True or false: Every time the prairie rattlesnake sheds its skin, a new rattle forms.

(Answer on page 64)

55

Raccoon

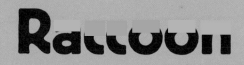

Diet: Nuts, berries, fruits, insects, eggs, grains, frogs, and fish

Weight: 20 pounds

Size: 3 feet long (including tail)

Location: North and South America

Raccoons can often be found outside of the forest near areas inhabited by humans. They are intelligent and crafty, finding their way into garbage cans and garages to find food.

Did You Know?

Sometimes called a "coon" for short, the raccoon is a small, nocturnal mammal with a ringed tail and black facial markings that look like an eye mask.

1

2

Fun Fact!

Raccoons have grizzled coats that range from tan and gray to silver and black. They have between 5 and 10 full rings around their bushy tails.

3

4

5

6

Rocky Mountain Goat

Details

Size: 40 inches tall at the shoulder
Weight: 200 to 250 pounds
Diet: Alpine furs, grasses, foliage, herbs, and lichens
Location: North America

Did You Know?

One or more times per year, Rocky Mountain goats travel to salt licks. These mineral deposits provide goats with important nutrients that supplement their vegetarian diet.

The Rocky Mountain goat has a coarse white coat, black horns, and a short beard. Their hoofed feet and strong legs make them great climbers on steep, rocky cliffs.

1

2

3

4

5

6

Fun Fact! Male goats have thick skin on the sides of their bodies that protects them from the sharp horns of other males. However, females are more aggressive than males and are known for being very protective of their young!

Red Fox

Size: 16 inches tall at the shoulder

Diet: Rodents, hares, rabbits, snakes, birds, eggs, and fruit

Weight: 10 to 15 pounds

Location: North America, Europe, Asia, North Africa, and Australia

Did You Know?

A red fox's coat is usually a dark reddish color, but it can also include white, black, and silver. The coat contains two layers: an underlayer of soft fur to keep warm, and an outer layer of coarse guard hairs to keep the fur dry.

The cunning red fox is a nocturnal canine with large, triangular ears; a pointed muzzle; a light ruff of cheek fur; and a bushy, white-tipped tail.

Mini Quiz

A baby fox can be called all of the following EXCEPT a...

A. Pup
B. Calf
C. Cub
D. Kit

(Answer on page 64)

Giant Panda

The giant panda is found in the wild only in China. An endangered animal, there are about 1,600 left in the wild.

Did You Know?

The giant panda is a large bear with a distinct black-and-white coat. These large creatures spend up to 16 hours a day eating!

1

2

3

4

Pandas are vocal animals that use chirps, barks, bleats, and honks to communicate a range of emotions and messages.

Fun Fact!

5

6

Mini Quiz Answers

Page 11: C. Barn owls can be white, yellow, and orange—but not black.

Page 13: False. Both male and female bighorn sheep have horns.

Page 21: E. Coyotes have a varied diet that includes a wide range of animals.

Page 27: D. Forest elephants can live to be 70 years old!

Page 31: False. The largest bear in the world is the Alaskan Kodiak bear.

Page 33: False. A hedgehog does not have spines on his face, underside, or limbs.

Page 37: A. Male and female mute swans are called "cobs" and "pens."

Page 55: True. A mature prairie rattlesnake sheds its skin one to two times a year. Each shedding results in a new rattle at the end of its tail!

Page 61: B. Baby foxes are most often called "kits," but they can also be called "pups" or "cubs."